BECOMING BEAUTIFUL

Also by Becca Lee

Pulling Petals

BECOMING BEAUTIFUL

A Collection of Poetry and Prose

by

BECCA LEE

Becoming Beautiful
Written and arranged by **Becca Lee**
ALL RIGHTS RESERVED

Cover art and design by **Mitch Green**

And, finally,
I will grow in all the places
that I've too long hid.

So, watch as I shed this skin
and become something
so much more beautiful
than flesh and bone could ever be.

Watch as I become me.

DEDICATION

When I write, I write for her…

Letters of happiness, truth and hope for the little me that I once knew; that little girl who changed my life even though she could not make sense of hers.

Every word I write is a tribute to her heart, courage and strength – an undying *thank you* to the little me that, despite all that she came to face, never gave up hope on the woman that I would become. Never stopped believing in all that she knew I could be.

The little me who helped me to learn the becoming beauty of imperfection and the power of forgiveness.

I write to her, for her and because of her.

To my baby girl Tylah Rose –

Thank you for showing me the true meaning of strength and proving that the human spirit is so much stronger than these fragile bodies we are gifted.

You have brought more love to my (our) life than you will ever know.

This is the story of my survival.
The blossoming of my heart.
The beginning of my ever after.
The tale of my becoming.

BECOMING

Dear human,

You are beautiful and you are treasure.
Do not let them tell you otherwise.

There is no right way to break, cope and heal,
so you must do so by any means that you can.

You are not maladaptive, dysfunctional or wrong.

You are human. You are perfectly imperfect.
You are learning. You are growing.

You are forever becoming and you are beautiful.

PHASES

Today, as with every day, is a new day.

Be sure to remind yourself
that it is okay to be different from yesterday
or not quite ready for tomorrow.

Sometimes we take a step back, regress,
and other times we *grow* more in one day
than we have in an entire year.

And that is exactly what life is all about –
balance and *change.*

For even the moon has its phases,
so why cannot we?

IT MATTERS NOT

I often question the woman I'd now be
if not for the bitter bite of pain
I grew to know so well
in those formative, oh so tender years
and the darkness in which I too long dwelt.
I wonder as to whether I am richer for my suffering
as I have so long told myself I am
or if that is merely a shallow blanket of lies
I have learned to drape over my shoulders
and across my chest
when the truth of the world (my past)
sits a little too cold upon the naked soft of my flesh.
But then I realize it matters not.
For my past is my past, my truths are my truths
and there is no changing the pages
that have already been scribed.
I am here now and this tale is still mine to shape.
So, I will stain the blank pages that remain
with ambition and empathy
and tell my story with unfaltering pride.

BUTTON BY BUTTON

Today I am undressing myself of these insecurities.

These uncertainties this world
has sown into my flesh
and that have taken root beneath my bones.

I am stripping myself of these surface labels
that do anything but define me
and embracing my entirety.

I am handing back the weight
of relentless comparison
and allowing my shoulders reprieve
from burdens not theirs to hold.

Today I am undressing myself of these insecurities
and stepping out into myself.

What a beautiful moment it is when you look into the mirror and find naught but kind, accepting eyes staring back at you. When pride has taken the place of shame and acceptance has replaced unending judgement. When you finally feel at peace (home) within the skin that encases you.

How liberating it is to see your naked, raw form and find a smile gracing your lips.

SOBER

When I begin to drown in memories of you and become intoxicated on the bottomless glass of *what ifs*, I find sobriety in the remembrance of all that you put me through. How that, even when I stood by you at your weakest, I was too much for you at my strongest.

WALK AWAY

If it is not healing your heart,
nourishing your soul
or helping you grow –
walk away.

Life is too short
and precious of a gift
to waste it
on that which is not destined to be.

LIONESS

You may have borrowed me,
held me temporarily
under your name and sway,
but you did not make me
and you will not break me –
I, and only I, can decide my fate.

REVERENCE

Like any work of art, she had created her life
bit-by-bit and piece-by-piece.

Gradually adding to herself here and there
as she went through life's journey –
realizing along the way
that it was her many contradictions
which made her beautiful in her own right.

For every blemish, mistake and lesson
had added depth and nuance to her being
and it was exactly those contrasts
that made her existence an exquisite masterpiece
that she was proud to call her own.

Χλοη

There is something truly
(breathtakingly) beautiful
about your painstaking honesty.
Your utter vulnerability
in the face of the world.

How you would rather burn at the stake
for your own admissions
than hold still your tongue
a moment longer.

And I cannot wait for the day
when you look into the pane's reflection
and find that all the comparison, contempt,
pain and insecurity
have melted away.

When you can look upon yourself
and say your name with pride.
When you can speak to the mirror
without bitter venom dripping from your lips
and falling to burn
the brilliant body that carries you.

That day is coming, my dear,
that day is nigh.

TIME

They say time heals all wounds
but whilst it may dull the pain
and blunt the edges
it cannot heal wholly on its own.
You, my dear, you must work with time.
You must tend your own wounds,
bandage the past
and stitch together your future.
Time alone is not enough,
but you, my dear, *you are.*

SHANGRI-LA

I am not a religious soul,
but fear not for me.

*I have faith enough
for all humanity.*

For I believe
not in something greater,
but in *everything.*

I believe in existence itself
and choose to love life
even at its worst.

So fear not for me,
for I am alive
and already living
in the paradise of my destiny.

SACRED

Darling, know that you are as a temple –
sacred and worthy of worship
even when you fall into ruin.

THE ART OF KEEPING

Remember, my darling,
the act of love is not the act of surrender.
Do not allow yourself to be lost in love
and lost you will not be.
Allow love to complement your all
but never, not even for a moment,
let it steal your luster.

Repeat after me:

The presence or absence of another does not define me and never will I let it. I, myself, am wholly complete and will forever remain, so long that I will it.

The presence or absence of another does not define me and never will I let it. I, myself, am wholly complete and will forever remain, so long that I will it.

The presence or absence of another does not define me and never will I let it. I, myself, am wholly complete and will forever remain, so long that I will it.

The presence or absence of another does not define me and never will I let it. I, myself, am wholly complete and will forever remain, so long that I will it.

The presence or absence of another does not define me and never will I let it. I, myself, am wholly complete and will forever remain, so long that I will it.

BEYOND

Do not let your heart
be caged by your body's bones,
nor your spirit
defined by the shell which holds it.

Crawl out of your skin's comfort
and blossom beyond
the limitations of your flesh.

You, my dear, are human
and you were not made to be contained –
for there is an entire universe
in motion within you.

THE PERFECT DISEASE PT.3

When the world saw her, this precious little butterfly, they gasped and spoke only of her beauty and 'perfection'– an insult that cut her to the very core and slowly began to threaten her very existence.

For she had not spent so many years developing inside her body's cocoon to be valued by something that she was not, nor could ever be.

And so, she took it upon herself to shed the very skin that they thought made her, bleeding away the perfect curse, until she was left bloodied, raw and wholly herself.

UNYIELDING GRACE

She carried ever her sadness
with unyielding grace,
for she knew that
the brilliant bloom of Spring
was nothing if not for
the timely death of Autumn's change.

And alike the wildflower you must rise up
out of the depths and darkness of your surrounds
to the glory of the light above,
but forever stay connected and true to your roots.

EQUALITY

Never place yourself above your fellow man,
for we are all, *each and every one of us,*
born of equal rights to the nourishing earth beneath
and the wonder of the stars above.

...And it is those
who place themselves upon pedestals
who have the farthest to fall.

If I have learned anything in my time,
anything at all,
it is that you learn as much
from each and every fall
as you do from your greatest successes.

So, bask in the warm Summer
of happiness and contentment
whilst they grace you with their presence,
but do not fear the cold chills of Winter's pain
nor the uncertainty of Autumn's change.

You must allow your heart
to swell, break and heal (more than once)
and be brave enough to trust,
forgive and trust again.

But, my dear, above all else,
you must live. For to truly live,
to be alive and experience life in its fullest,
well... that is the greatest gift of all

STAINED-GLASS HEART

"Here..." she said, baring her stained-glass heart in outstretched hands, *"it is yours if only you have the courage to take it, the strength to hold it and the patience to keep it. It's not perfect, I know — it has been chipped and cracked, but I promise you that it is not broken. It still beats with passion and love aplenty. It is the most resplendent part of me and the light it holds within shines all the brighter for the times and places that it has been worn thin. So, it is yours, if only you have the courage to take it, the strength to hold it and the patience to keep it..."*

BEAUTIFUL CONTRADICTIONS

She was as delicate as Spring's first blossom, yet as resilient as the ancient oaks that tower above – the most beautiful contradiction that I have ever seen. Born with a wild heart and a peaceful soul, she knew her place in the world and would never settle for less than she deserved, even if it meant standing against the odds and fighting to keep true to the beat of her heart.

With a presence as gentle as the stillest water and a spirit which burned with a passion more voracious than the wildest sea, she was so much more than simply the sum of her past. So, do not make the mistake of underestimating all that she is or forgetting to appreciate her in her entirety – for extraordinary beauty can be found in that which is chaotic and imperfect if only you have the courage to open your heart and mind to such possibility.

She might not always make perfect sense, or any sense at all for that matter, and she certainly won't fit into all the spaces and places that the world has set out for her, but don't you dare try and change her or save her. The only hero she needs in this life is herself. She is the epitome of everything unrefined and pure in this world – *the most beautiful contradiction that I have ever seen and holding within her a world of possibilities.*

ARTEM

I have been fractured, chipped and broken –
but never have I fallen to pieces
beyond the capacity of my own repair.

And the most beautiful part of it all,
is that I would not have it any other way.

For you see, I came into this world
a blank canvas, and, when my time comes,
I will be leaving it as a masterpiece
that has been magnificently marred
by all of life's wonders.

*Never again would she let herself forget the utter
frozenness of apathy. What it meant to be numb. The
ultimate sacrifice. For a life bereft of living, feeling,
falling, soaring is fit for none. She was alive and that
meant taking the good with the bad, the smiles with the
tears, the wins with the falls and bleeding, forever
bleeding, for what she loved.*

DESIRES

Eyes once filled
with excitement and longing
now look at me
only with complacency –
the boredom of familiarity.

But I am no china doll
made to be placed in a safe corner,
thrown sporadic glances and never touched –
to be admired but never truly loved.

No. No. No.

I am flesh and I am blood.
My heart beats and my body longs.

I desire to be desired,
I want to be wanted,
I love to be loved
and if you think that I am willing to settle
for comfort in place of passion,
you, my dear, are sorely, sorely mistaken.

It is a slow and painful dying
this watching of complacent eyes.
This watching someone fall out of love.

For complacency becomes the death
of all things wonderful.

SILENT TRUTHS

"Silent..."

A word that for far too long defined my existence. For I once thought my silence necessary – a depiction of my strength and a stoic demonstration of what I could endure alone.

But I realize now how naive I was.

For it takes more strength to admit you are struggling than it does to suffer quietly, more courage to ask for help than it does to remain voiceless as you drown in an ocean of despair and more valor to speak out against injustice than it does to sit by and passively allow its perpetuation.

So, no longer will I remain silent when my voice needs to be heard. *I will speak out and I will speak truths.*

I have been silent too long, but silent I shall be no more. *For my voice is a gift and my story is my legend, so silent I shall be no more.*

KINDNESS

Be kind to your body,
gentle with your mind
and patient with your heart.

You are still becoming, my dear,
and there is no one else more deserving
of the nurturing grace of your love.

DESERVING

I have been given things that I did not yet deserve and held onto them longer than I should have. Been selfish in luck and too often taken it for granted.

When I first found you I did not deserve you, I knew it, but still on and on I desperately clung. And when I lost you I knew it was meant to be, but still I was not ready nor prepared. Still I did not want to let go.

Clinging. Clinging. Clinging.

But I suppose that is the true definition of selfishness– clinging greedily to that which was never meant for us out of fear of facing the harsh truth of reality.

Losing you was the hardest thing I've ever had to face, but the greatest lesson I have ever learned. For it taught me that if I wanted something so beautiful, so pure and so seamless, that I best become a person deserving of such utter magnificence.

And so, I became someone deserving of not only the love of another, but of something so much more valuable and irreplaceable – *someone deserving of myself.*

When you open your mouth
and unfurl your tongue
do not whisper to me the impossible
promise of forever.
I have no interest in such fables.
Promise me instead your today,
your absolute entirety today,
and the rest will remain unwritten.

INEXORABLE

There is none better equipped in this life to
appreciate the brilliant light birthed forth
from enduring and unrelenting hope
than those who have known the darkness of despair
and once lived in the seemingly bottomless
chasm of dejection.

AUTHOR

Your destiny is bound
only by your choices.

So, ask yourself this –
are you willing to play slave to fate
or will you stand up and shape
the future you want and deserve?

For if you are not willing to work
for what you want
and fight for what you desire,
you best be prepared to settle for much less.

You are not a passive character
in the story of your life,
you are the author
and only you can decide your fate.

NEW DAY, NEW LIGHT

I have been crippled beneath the weight
of shattered self-esteem
and held prisoner within the confines
of these insecurities.

I have apologized for what I am
and begged for forgiveness for what I am not.

I have given this world the power
to make me feel less than I am (nothing)
and torn myself apart to save others the bother.

I have kept self-depreciation
as a long-term bedfellow
and forgotten what it feels like
to sleep with the peace of contentment.

But times are changing. I am changing.
I am growing, learning, evolving.
I am becoming what I always was
and shedding what was never meant to be me.

But it isn't always easy.
There are days that I slip into the ways
of times a past, but still will I keep trying
to see myself in the light and truth of this new day
rather than through the shroud of these eyes
who have forever been known to lie.

EVOLVING

I've come so far and achieved so much,
but the best part of it all
is that this is only the beginning.

I will never stop growing –
for my evolution is eternal and
I am forever becoming.

FIREWORK

Never forget that,
alike the stars above,
as long as you live
your light will never cease to burn –
even when you can't see it.

And sometimes it takes
the darkest of moments
for us to realize
exactly how brightly we can shine.

I promise to love you
for as long as my lungs swell with air –
today, tomorrow and every day
that I come to see.

For you are the most perfectly beautiful reason
I have ever had to breathe.

Every time
I think I am not strong enough to do this
she finds a way to show me that I am.

WILD ONE

Wild One,
they will try and tame your heart
and clip your glorious wings –
for some people in this world
wish to subdue that which they do not understand
and repress that which they are envious of.

But please do not fear them
nor hold the burden of abhorrence within you.
You will only fuel their ignorance
and extinguish the essence
of what makes you so rare, beautiful and pure.

Wild One,
you were not born with malice in your heart
nor a spiteful mind,
so do not let them plant those dark seeds within you.
Never surrender your truths
simply so that you may fit inside their cages.

Being true to yourself
and living in peace
is proof enough that you are
as you were meant to be.

So please do not change for them
nor let them change you.
Stay true, Wild One,
please stay true to you.

WOMAN

My curves are carved
from the greatest of mountains
and my heart born
from the depths of the deepest seas.

My mind is a chasm
of unfathomable possibility
and my soul old
as existence itself.

I am more than this shell.
I am human.
I am the bearer of new life.
I am worthy.

I am limited only by the constraints
I place upon myself.

I am woman.

THE BUTTERFLY EFFECT

The world appreciated her beauty, admired it even, but it never truly respected her – never saw her as anything more than an aesthetic miracle.

To them she was too fragile, too passive, too beautiful to be anything more than a prized possession – like a porcelain doll hidden high upon a dusty shelf to be longingly looked at but never truly loved.

Oh, but how blind their ignorance made them. Little did they know all that she was – all that she was capable of.

For it takes profound strength to remain so magnificently delicate in what can be, at times, such a callous world. In a system of self-induced chaos, they could not see that she was the deterministic variable– the one who could change it all.

Only she knew the perturbation that her silent flutter could effect if only she desired it so…

And it was her decision not to, that made her all the more powerful.

CRAVEN

Whispering echoes scream your name
as I lie naked and bound in the lonely cell of my bed,
the sheets tangled around me,
restraining me,
in the attempt to keep
some semblance of your touch.
But despite the pain of losing you,
I realize now that I was alone long before you left.
I was merely holding onto the memory
of something you never were –
loving a ghost of what I thought we could be.
For you never loved me,
not truly.
And you never will.
You were simply in love with the idea of being loved
but the reality of it was too much for you.
I was too much.
I gave too much.
I set your soul ablaze
and ignited passion within your heart,
but you were so used to the cold
that you couldn't help but drown our love
in the hope of saving yourself
the pain of being burned.

ACETOUS

Oh, sweet love,
how bitter you fall
when bestowed
upon a heart unworthy.

HERE I AM

I've not always been this way, you see, so content (at home) within this skin and at peace with this painstakingly poetic life.

You see, there were years (a lifetime's worth) when everything was shrouded in an impenetrable darkness and the only light that ever slipped through was designed to burn (never to warm). A time when my own thoughts were my worst enemy and I was trapped within a prison of my own creation. A time when hope was a foreign tongue.

Yet, despite it all, here I am, standing before you in the glorious (warming) light of a new dawn. Here I am bathed in forgiveness and dressed in acceptance.

But this newfound warmth and light are not where I always reside. For there are still barren days. Days when my bones are too brittle to hold the weight of my heart. Days when my gait is more limp than stride.

Yet, despite it all, here I am. Here I am.

DICHOTOMY

Oh, my darling daughter,
this world will ask a great many things of you.
Difficult things.
Impossible things.
It will ask you to be meek yet certain,
to have a voice yet hold your tongue,
to be an equal that is willing to subserve,
to be delicate but not cracked,
to be easy to swallow but not too dilute.
But I tell you this –
within you is passion enough
to engulf this world
and the strength and depth
of the fathomless ocean.
So, do not bend to their wills, my love.
Don't you dare.
Stand strong and stay true
for you are exactly as you are meant to be
and within you is everything and all
you will ever need.

CORPOREAL

Loving you taught me that infinity is inadequate
when compared to the beauty of morality.

ENCHANTRESS

She finds wonder in the mundane,
has hope despite what she has faced
and sees beauty in the insipid.

It is just the way she is.

To her, the world is magic
and life the most precious of gifts.

IT IS TIME

It is time, my love, it is time...
Time to let the past be laid to rest and make peace
with that which is not within your control.

Exonerate your heart for the times it has bled for
people who were not yet ready or worthy of your love
and forgive your mind for placing the happiness of
others above your own value and worth.

Understand that we all drift from the path and get
lost from time to time, but know that never are we too
far gone to find ourselves – to rediscover our true
beings as we venture through this tempestuous
journey of life, love and loss.

You must learn to welcome the unexpected as readily
as the planned and let go of the burdens you have too
long held so that you may finally give your shoulders
reprieve from carrying the dead weight of times of
yore.

Be mindful of what you allow to grow
in your heart, my dear.
It has but only four chambers within
and each beat is as precious as the last.

Becca Lee

SEASONS

Do not fall in love
with the glorious bloom of my flowers
if you will not, cannot,
nourish the depths of my roots.

*(Remember, pretty decays, my dear, but the foundation
of a beautiful heart and soul are forever.)*

Too many had fallen in love
with the pretty of her flesh's flowers
and not the depth of her roots.

And, so, she took it upon herself
to pluck each petal,
one by one,
until she was left bare of adornment
and wholly herself.

Until she became beautiful
in the only way that truly matters.

PRIDE

I see you.

I see beneath that smile you wear for the world
(the one you paint on with every sunrise
and bleed away each night).

I see you drowning
in the dark depths of your sorrow
and bending beneath the weight
of your shattered heart.

I know you see it too,
each and every time you stare into the mirror
and see those depthless eyes burning back at you –
those deceitful eyes devoid of anything
but insecurity and hopelessness.

But you see,
I see so much more than just that.
I see you coming up to steal breaths
between each crashing wave
and piecing your pieces back together
each and every morn.

I see you waging an impossible war against yourself
and standing still,
fighting still.

I see you, my dear, the real you.
The utter glory of your resilience and will.

I see you and I want you to know that never (ever)
have I held such admiration for another
nor witnessed such raw beauty.

I see you and oh, how I love you

MUSINGS

Who is this woman who stands before me
in the cool reflection of mirrored glass?

Tell me please,
for although she looks vaguely familiar
I do not recognize her
now that the panes show no pain.

Lost is the slouch of shoulders
crippled beneath the weight of dejection
and filled is the hollow sorrow
from beneath the hazel of her eyes.
Vanished are the bones
who so desperately craved to show their glory
through leather skin stretched too thin
and finally, there is supple flesh
that is accepted rather than cut back.

Please someone, anyone,
tell me tales of this woman before me,
for although I do not recognize her
of this I am certain,
she looks vaguely familiar
and she feels a whole lot like destiny.

It takes great courage to love yourself in a world
that is constantly trying to find ways
to tell you not to.

TOXICITY

This isn't what we once knew –
the love we thought we had.
Unshakable.
Unbreakable.
It is more fragile than we ever thought possible.
More mortal than we dare to admit.
Finite.
Gone.
It is now simply a question
of how much longer we choose
to cling to hollow cages
and scream into the silence
where there once was a living beat.
How much longer we will be white knuckled
and hoarse voiced from this feeble attempt
to cling onto what once was.
From trying to breathe life
back into what has long since passed.
This isn't what we once knew
and there is only so much longer
that I can keep inhaling the toxic waste
that is our decaying love.

PERPETUAL EPHEMERA

One of the most beautifully tragic truths
you will come to know
is that there are some people
who will forever remain in your heart
even when they do not remain in your life.

DUALITY

I shelter the world from the truth
for I have forever been the protector,
the happiness,
the strength.

But, oh how I long for the times
that I can be the victim,
the sorrow,
the weakness.

How I long to be human without expectations
and to feel without restraint –
to show my true colors
(the bright and dark alike)
and be loved all the same.

It is the loneliest of fates
hiding behind a forever smile.

Becca Lee

PHOENIX

She had grown so much in the past few years
that she hardly recognized the girl she once was
and barely remembered the pain
for which she had shed so many crimson tears.

But the funny thing was,
she wasn't someone else now –
she was more herself
than she had even known, felt and been.

Years that had once seemed
unending and insufferable, suddenly made sense –
for she realized that they were preparing her
for a rebirth of magnificent proportions.

She wasn't just a caterpillar
that had become a butterfly.
No. She was a single atom
that had become an entire universe
in and of herself.

A remarkable and beautiful force
to be reckoned with.

PRIDE

Wear your skin with pride.
Your bones will grow weary
beneath the weight
of shattered self-esteem
for you, my dear,
were not made to live in shame.

RECOGNITION

Oh softness, how I used to detest thee.
Trying so desperately to hide you
as I rubbed steel-wool against my palms
and walked the most tumultuous paths
on the barest of soles.
Sheltering my insides beneath stone
and keeping the cage of my ribs locks and bound
from fear my rose-colored insides
were too delicate for this life
(that I was too delicate for this life).
I tried so hard to hide those parts of me,
tried even harder to be anything but me.
But now I understand my softness is a strength
and my tenderness a gift.
I was blessed with a dandelion heart,
which is to say I was born to spread this love.
Which is to say
I am more beautiful for the shattering.
So, I will scrape away this calloused skin
and hand over the key to my heart's cage
as I stand here before you bare, beautiful
and wholly worthy of this tender love and life.

BLOOMING WITHIN

Here, take my pretty,
I need it not.
For I have learned to grow beyond,
and blossom beneath,
this prison of flesh
that too long defined me.
I have, finally, become beautiful
in my entirety
and grown in all the places
I too long hid.

So here, take my pretty,
I need it not.

NEVER AGAIN

How little I must have felt
to try and convince you to stay
(to feel as though I needed you
when you didn't even want me).

Never again. Never again. Never again.

Never again will I allow myself to become so small
in the shadow of another
when I too have my own light.

For I do not belong on knees bent
begging for scraps.

No. No. No.

I belong on steady feet
confident from all
they have already carried me through
in this life.

I belong to myself, I know that now,
and never again will I allow
the presence or absence of another
to define my happiness or worth.

There is strength to be found in our solitude
and wisdom to be learned from our weathered
but still beating hearts.

Becca Lee

TENDER

From this day forth
I promise to speak only gentle words
of tender adulation to myself
after having too long let
the bitter venom of loathe
drip forth from my lips
upon this body of mine.
I am responsible for loving myself
first, foremost and entirely.

And so, I will sow the seeds of love
beneath this skin of mine
and nurture them with the kindness
I've so long denied my deserving self.

A LIFETIME OF PAIN OVERDUE

What I've learned
in my ~~tender~~ brutal years upon this earth:
there is undeniable magic in hope,
becoming beauty in imperfection
and unfathomable power in forgiveness.

So, Love I Will

This body has harbored the greatest treasure
and born to me the gift of life.
No longer can I look upon it with contempt
no matter how hard old habits try to die.

This flesh is a prison of insecurity no more.

This body (my body)
has been the vessel of mighty creation
and bestowed me with a limitless
legacy of love. So, love I will.

HOLDING OUT

After finally realizing the power
of what it was to be kind to herself
and patient with her heart,

to love herself after so many years
of underestimating her worth
and doubting her very existence,

she swore that never again
would she give her heart
to one who promised to love her
despite her shortcomings and imperfections.

Instead, she would wait,
regardless of how long,
for the one who would truly love her
because of her everything.

"Vulnerability is strength" ...

She whispered to herself
as mascara bled from her face.

*"Embrace the pain — for it will shape you and, in turn,
you will become forever greater than that which
threatens to stand in your way.*

*So, fall down, bleed, break and cry ... do whatever it is
that you must, but don't you dare give up."*

STILL ME

Yesterday, you told me
that you no longer recognized me –
distaste spilling from your mouth
as if this was a truth
that I should somehow find shame in.

Only, I know better now.
Finally, I know better.
For you see, I am still me.

It is just that when we were together
I was made a little more of "sorries"
than I was of myself,
I was a little more doormat
than backbone
and I was a little more weed
in your garden of self-proclaimed Eden
than I was a beautiful, blooming wildflower.

You say that I've changed,
that I am no longer the person
you once considered loving.

But words designed to cut me down
to the ground beneath your feet
(down where you kept me
so neatly trimmed all those years)
fall instead as sweet liberation upon my ears.

You are right,
I am not the same reflection
you once threw your scraps of love at.
But not because I am someone else now.

No.

Because I am finally (finally) the me
I too long let wither
in your ego's shadow.

Because, finally,
I have stepped into the light
and allowed myself the chance to bloom.

MOSAIC APPRECIATION

I am learning to hold my pieces with humble hands
and beginning to understand that parts of myself
are better left in my own disarray
than rebuilt into another's perfection.

It is liberating, you see,
this holding without needing to fix.
This feeling (wholly and utterly) without drowning.
This mosaic appreciation.

This looking (seeing) and smiling.

VIRTUES

The landscape of my body
is a forever changing canvas,
but the raw beauty beneath
never falters or fades.

So, don't you dare judge me
by that which is arbitrary and transient,
for it is what is hidden within
that makes me truly beautiful
in my own right, virtue and prowess.

THE GIRL WHO KNEW BETTER THAN TO WISH UPON THE STARS

She had no need to gaze at the stars, for she knew they gazed upon her – forever envious of the life upon earth she was gifted with.

So many wished endlessly upon those stars, forgetting the doomed fate of which so many of them had already met – forever burning for everything but themselves until they collapse, exhausted, into nothing more than a brilliant memory destined to be brutally forgotten the moment another dares to shine that little bit brighter.

But not her. She had learned that her head wasn't meant to live in the clouds. No. Her feet were blessed to kiss the earth and she knew the importance of being grounded, for whilst wings may take you away from the pain, roots can hold you strong enough to endure it.

She knew better. She knew to be thankful for each breath she was gifted with and every beat of her heart– whether it be heavy or filled with joy. She knew the blessing it was to be alive. To feel.

So no, she did not gaze nor wish upon them, for she knew that the strength to live, to achieve and to flourish lay firmly within her reach and that no amount of wishing could take the place of dedication, persistence and unwavering hope. But more than anything she knew that even the stars coveted the smolder of life in her amber eyes.

CONTRIVED FALLACIES

My body is merely a vessel,
my face a distraction.
Superficial facades.
I yearn for someone to look
beyond my flesh
and beneath my bones –
for someone to look at me
in all my twisted glory
and smile at what they find
hidden within.

EARS UNWORTHY

Today I promise myself that
"I'm sorry"
will not spill freely from these lips.
Will not fall upon ears unworthy.
Today I promise myself that
I will be unapologetic
in all my tarnished glory.

CHOICES

Today I choose to forgive myself
for past mistakes.

Today I choose happiness,
contentment and inner-peace.

Today I choose to free myself of negativity
and to take ownership of my life.

Today, and every day, I choose self-love
and to believe in the magic of undying hope.

GRATITUDE

Be grateful, always. Even if for nothing more than the continued rise of the sun and fall of the moon, for appreciation unburdens the heart and allows the soul to breathe wholly. And it is only when you learn to see this life as the gift it truly is, that you will finally know what it is to be at peace within yourself and the world that surrounds you.

I am building a house
that is more than four walls.
It will be a palace of love,
a chapel of forgiveness
and a temple of respect.
It will be a masterpiece of fractured grace
and a tribute to humble beginnings.
I am building a home within this body.

I am building me.

This is my home you see,
and I will no longer
let it be a place of shame
or a vessel of insecurity

BECOMING BEAUTIFUL

She buries the sorrows
of the world beneath her flesh
and bares the wounds
of her solicitude with pride –
content within the perfect knowledge
that nothing can fracture
what has already survived being broken.

And so, I smile
as I look upon her creases and cracks,
for the beauty of morality burns within her.

A beauty that is not born into this world,
but rather one that is suffered for,
earned and become –
the beauty of a heart and soul
so deeply scarred by compassion
that all else becomes insignificant
by its comparison.

THANK YOU

Thank you for walking away when mascara stained my cheeks and my self-worth crumpled beneath me as I begged you please stay.

For despite the bitter pain of losing you, the realization that I have need of no other but myself was the most profoundly liberating truth and, in your absence, finally was I able to realize my worth.

TENDER HEART

…and perhaps happiness
is simply knowing
that all the inevitable pain
is forever worth
the gift of a tender heart.

BATTLEGROUND

I will hold this body tender
after years too many
spent callously rending it apart
and stroke this skin with adulation
as I learn to treasure
the Braille tales of survival it has to tell.
For my body, this body,
is uniquely mine to love and cherish
and I will no longer let it be
my battleground.

You deserve love.
The unyielding kind that is born only from within –
from betwixt the still beating chambers of your heart.
The kind that knows no bounds.

You deserve peace.
The unwavering kind that washes over you each day–
constant waves of calm drawing out uncertainty in
the morn and returning only tranquility in the eve.
The kind that nurtures and heals.

And you, my dear, deserve happiness.
The resilient kind that knows the transient nature of
pain and despair and never loses hope
for it is stronger than all you will come to face.
The kind that will see you safely through this life.

I hope that one day *(soon)* you will realise this
and *(finally)* know that it is all within your reach.

ALL OF YOU

I see you,
all of you –
the beauty,
the grim,
the chaos
and the glory –
and please know
(even if there is nothing else of which you are certain)
that there is not one part of you
that I do not love
with everything
and all that I am.

Unbutton your heart and undress your soul
and come to me in your naked grace;
stripped back of pretense
and unembellished by concealment.

Bare of all but yourself.

I beg of you to expose your raw, dark and broken
so that I may show those pieces of you love
until you become devoid of insecurity –

until you do not know how to do anything
but love yourself.

MARROW

Oh Darling,
if it is my heart that you seek
you must learn to close your eyes
and open your mind.

For I am so much more
than meets your sight
and I will not settle
for skin-deep desires.

I have want only for a love so profound
that it crawls beneath my skin
and buries itself within
the cage of my bones.

*A love that becomes a part of my being
and cherishes me in my entirety.*

Darling,
undress me of this skin
(this pretense)
and discover the universes
I hold hidden within.

MYOPIA (BLINDNESS IN SIGHT PT. 2)

Through her eyes the world moved – silent, detached and ignorant. A grey blur which passed with such individual conformity that it became nothing more than a choreographed performance, with each motion rehearsed again and again, over and over, in the screaming silence of one's mind. For perfection was the only desire, yet remained all but attainable.

Yet in closing her eyes and opening her mind she was able to bring a dead world back to life. Behind the black shroud of sight, she watched the world move – peaceful, beautiful and warm. A colored blur which passed with such striking individuality that she could not help but fall in love with the inexplicable beauty that it held.

For you see, to seek that which feeds the soul rather than the eye is to know true contentment and understand the meaning of beauty.

The world moves silent, detached and ignorant only because our frivolity and self-proclaimed privilege leave us too blind to seek the beauty it truly holds in the depths of its soul.

*Too often are we drawn to the loud, vivid places —
the places of grandeur and spectacle. And whilst it is
important to know these places, you must also take the
time to seek out the quiet places and learn to relish the
simplest of gifts, whether it be the gentle touch of the sun
or the soft song of the whispering wind. I beg of you to
seek the calm and tender as readily as the majestic. To
find magic in the smallest of events and embrace the
velvet ink of darkness as avidly as you crave the light
which forever finds a way to pierce it.*

OCEAN HEART

Come,
explore the uncharted territories
of my soul
and delve into the pretty chaos
of my ocean heart,
for it is only once you've come to know
the darkest corners of my mind
and uncovered the deepest caverns of my being
that I will let you speak
the sweet words of love
and not a moment before.

Call me selfish if you will,
but I am not the type of girl
who is willing to give herself as sacrifice
in the name of love.

I love wholly, fiercely and fervently
but I am simply not willing to lose myself
in order to gain parts of another.

RATIONALE

"You don't know what you've got until it's gone…"

No.
You did.

You always knew what you had – from the very first moment you found it, right up until the second that you lost it. You knew, and that is exactly why it is gone. If it had been enough, if I had been right and if it had been a chaotic harmony that engulfed your very sense… well, my dear, then it would still be here. But it wasn't enough, it wasn't right and it certainly didn't make you question reality and believe in everything extraordinary. As good as it was, it was always missing something. Always lacking that certain spark you could never quite put your finger on – that raw intensity of something purely primal and destined to be. So, trust me, you knew exactly what you had… it is just now that it is gone you have found that little bit of discomfit that unsettles your mindless complacency – which is exactly what was missing in the first place.

WITHOUT YOU

It may have taken me longer to realize
than I quite like to admit,
but without you I am still me –
as whole and beautiful as ever.
As much as I was before you
and as much as I was with you.

As much as I will always be.

UNSPOKEN

I have my untold stories.

The pages of my book I choose to keep hidden from the world. Not from shame – *never from shame* – but simply because there are pieces of me that I am not yet ready to gift to another. Pieces of me that I hold sacred within my heart's heart and worship for the unique treasure they truly are.

LUSTER

*I will not yield
to the harshness of this world
nor let the storms of life
steal this shine.*

THE STORY OF MY SURVIVAL

The story of my survival isn't a glamorous one –
it isn't made up of "once upon a times"
and "happily ever afters".

It doesn't roll off the tongue with sweet metaphors
or come with the invitation of batting lids.
Rather, it is told through gritted teeth
and bloodshot eyes.
It is pulled,
dragged,
forced
through white clenched fists
as I try and hold it back from ears
too delicate to understand
that it is more bloodied knees
than petticoat curtseys.

More self-depreciation and loathing
than self-respect and pride.
More "I'm sorry"
than the unapologetic tale it should have been.

You see,
I was made more from the blood and scars
than the smiles and sunshine.
I was shaped by misery
and crafted by dismay.

But the one flicker of hope,
the one ray of sunshine through it all
was a little girl,
the little me who refused to give up –
who dusted her knees,
licked the blood from still open wounds
and smiled through the tears.

For she knew.
Somehow, she knew
that she was destined for greater things.
Destined for stories worthy of pages
and the ears of hopeful hearts.

Becca Lee

UNDENIABLE

I am pulling back the skin from these bones
(this prison of flesh)
to allow myself room to bloom anew
without the constraint
of this meaningless superficial.
Stripping it all back so that I may blossom
into something truly worth beholding.
Something more than meets the eye.
Something so much deeper than your surface gaze.
Something profound, deep
and wholly undeniable.

Do not ignore
a beautiful mind,
spirit and heart
because of a beautiful face.
Do not discount
one's capacity
to be more
than meets the eye.

VENERATION

There will always be great admiration
for those who manage to survive
all of life's trials and tribulations –
but something greater is reserved for those
who do not just survive,
but who learn how to bud, bloom and flourish
against all odds.

Grow from your mistakes
(each and every one)
until you blossom
to your utmost potential...

OF MY FLESH AND BLOOD

Look at you —
you glorious disaster of fractured limbs,
torn skin and bruised organs.

Look at you breathing,
beating,
surviving.

Look at you still here.

Is that not proof enough
you are winning this fight;
that this battle is still yours to wage?

Look at you rising with the sun each morn
even when it may be clouded from sight —
even when the sky is more ashen memories
than soothing cerulean promises.

Look at you breathing
despite the suffocation of despair
hanging thick around your head
and beating despite the stifling weight of the world
sitting upon your chest.

And, my dear, look at you standing
even with this all upon your shoulders
and trying its best
to break the spirit of your back.

Look at you.
My goodness, look at you.
You are beautiful.
You are strength.
You are power.

TONGUE TIED

I find myself biting my tongue
more and more these days.
Holding back the watered words,
as I try to turn the delicate petals
that adorn my heart into thorns.
As I try and become someone
hard enough to withstand this love.
I am trying.
For you, I am trying.
But the more I try, the more I wonder –
Is it worth it? *Are you worth it....*

NOT MINE

I am stepping out from beneath old skin
and unburdening my shoulders
of the weight of unending comparison.

For you see,
these fears,
these inadequacies,
these insecurities,
they are not mine, not truly.

They belong to a world
consumed by the superficial
when I am born only of real –
real flesh and real blood.

I was not made to carry such sorrows in my bones.

So, I will step out from beneath this old skin
and learn to live with only love and graciousness
as I begin to see this glorious life
through fresh eyes and an eternally open heart.

INTERNAL WARFARE

The greatest obstacle you will face in this life
is yourself, my dear –
the doubt woven throughout your mind
and the fear harbored within your heart.

But do not allow them to stifle your dreams
or steal away your hope.
You must learn to embrace the chaos
so that it may become your peace
and find the courage to take chances
even when the stars are not perfectly aligned.

For this life will never be completely absent
of uncertainty and turbulence
but it may be absent
of utter dismay and hopelessness
when you find a way to work with your pain
so that you may forever learn and grow.

The most beautiful lesson I have learned
is the importance of touching my body with fingers
designed to hold rather than burn.

SORRY (NOT SORRY)

I am sorry that I was not enough for you
but enough I am
and enough I will forever be.

It was the moment that I froze
from the empty chill of loneliness,
whilst still in the warmth of your embrace,
that I realized that your promises of forever
were as hollow as your heart.

BLOSSOMING BEYOND

She did not believe in living life on the side lines or not taking chances in case she fell – for she knew that taking no risks was the greatest risk of all.

She was the type of girl who would rather gather the battle-scars of life, victory and loss, learning from both the wins and the falls, than to remain perfectly unblemished and wholly ignorant. And whilst she was completely open to the possibility of magic, she held her feet firmly on the ground – knowing that having hope and believing was only half the battle and hard work, dedication and courage made up the rest.

And so, she lived life as it was meant to be lived – to the fullest and with the utmost respect for herself and others. It did not matter than she was not everyone's idea of "right" and, frankly, she was thankful that she wasn't – *for she was purely and honestly herself and that is its own kind of perfection.*

To her it wasn't about fitting in or standing out, it was simply about being true, wholeheartedly and contentedly, to the entirety of her being.

And so, the only path she chose to take in life was the path that her heart and soul led her on, because deep down she knew that some rules were made to be broken and sometimes you need to fall before you can learn how to fly.

PERSPECTIVE

Learn to look at the familiar
with the wonder of fresh eyes
and open your heart
to seeing the world anew.

For when you do,
you may be surprised
at just how beautiful everything
you have always thought to be
insipid and mundane
can truly be.

Perceptions shape reality
and not all is as it may first appear.

So never stop searching for, and believing in,
all the beauty hidden within this world.

RESIDUE

Moments are exactly that – *moments.*

They were never meant to last.

You may savor them, recall them,
and treasure their remnants,
but never allow yourself
to fall into the delusion
of believing that that they
were meant to be forever.

For that, my dear,
is the most dangerous of traps.

RED BLOODED WOMAN

"Treat her like a queen..."

I am so sick of hearing these words.

If you love me,
do not treat me as though I were royalty –
for there is nothing romantic about a contrived,
filtered and restrained love.

I am not refined, polished nor proper.

No.

I am real, raw and tarnished.

Cut me and I promise you that I bleed red not blue.

So, love me only for the unique woman that I am
and treat me exactly as I deserve.

FALLIBLE

Be hungry for the truth.
Do not simply accept the dulcet lies of this world
put forth and repeated by easily satiated minds.

Search for the veracity hidden in myth
and dissolve the sweet fallacies
that are too often disguised as bitter truths.

Forever question,
for complacency is the bedfellow
of mediocrity.

REINCARNATION

Picking herself up and dusting herself off,
she stood taller than ever before –
finally tasting fresh air within her lungs
and allowing her heart and soul to become nourished
by nothing more than the beauty of the world
that surrounded her.

It was as if she had never truly lived
before this point –
as if she had been reborn into and of herself.

She began to breathe, love, rejoice and dream.

And for the first time
in what had seemed like an eternity,
she smiled truthfully and breathed freely
as she fell wholeheartedly in love with existence.

After so many years of fighting
what seemed to be an ever-losing battle
it simply took allowing herself the grace
of falling to pieces
for everything to fall (im)perfectly into place.

Stumbling.
Falling.
Bleeding.
Kneeling
Standing.
Healing.

This is how we grow.

DEPTHS

They tell you that you are too much —
that you feel this life too deeply
and live with too much fire.
But, my dear, heed not their words
nor try contain the wild flowing within you.
Know that I love you
as much when you are a raging ocean
as when you are the stillest of still seas;
that I cherish the dark depths of your soul
over any shallow waters of your surface.

SPIRIT

Even when her body was cast in midnight shadows
and bright screams of scarlet wept from her open soul,
she was still the most beautifully resilient creature
of whom I could ever dream.

For she was beaten, but not defeated.
Never defeated.

Every fall was simply a chance to rise again –
to prove her strength and worth,
and to become something stronger than before.

Oh darling, didn't you know that it takes much more
than the pitiable weakness of another
to break the spirit of a woman?

Becca Lee

There is endless beauty to be found
in the seemingly mundane
and limitless lessons to be learned
from the most painful of falls.

VITRUVIAN

To me, faith is the greatest of gifts,
but I find myself disheartened
by the fact that faith has become
synonymous solely with religion –
for what an ugly conflation that is indeed.
I, myself, am not a religious soul,
but I bare no ill will or misgivings to those who are.
I simply think that first and foremost,
and above all else,
we need to have faith in ourselves –
faith in tarnished beauty that is humanity.

My White Whale

My darling girl,

I am not perfect. Far from it in fact. A lesson too late learned in my life, but knowledge I finally welcome rather than deny.

A truth I hope that you will know forever within your heart. For nor are you and never shall you be.

You see, perfect is an unattainable desire. A white whale that will haunt your every waking breath and remain all but within your grasp. An iron shackle that will hold you back from the life you are destined to lead. A burden I hope you will never have to carry.

So, hear not their words when they tell you so. Know within yourself that you are something more than this infallible fallacy. You are human. You are made of flesh and (my) blood.

You will fall and you will bleed. You will know the bitter taste of failure and make mistakes aplenty. But do not fear them. Welcome them as readily as the times made of lavender skies and sunlight smiles.

For all my mistakes and all my flaws have led me here. Have gifted me with you. Have led to this becoming. To this complete contentment and love.

And too will you know the wonder of open skies and of possibilities opening with every step. For you will rise each time you fall and, no matter how long it takes, you will find wisdom and beauty in your scars.

Oh, my darling girl, if I can teach you nothing else in this life please let me teach you this. You are not perfect and within that knowledge may you find your true self and embrace yourself in your entirety.

HOLD ON

Do not let them strip you
of your tenderness, my love.
Softness is a virtue
too often surrendered
in the face of adversity.
Hold onto it. *Hold on.*

Try as you may you cannot break this softness.
I will forever be that wide-eyed, believing girl
who sees the world through rose-colored eyes.
For you see, this softness, it is me.

GIFTS

Darling, adorn yourself
with the jewels of self-love,
bathe in the cleansing waters of forgiveness
and give your soul permission to shine.
You are worthy.

Oh my, you are worthy.

Star Gazing

Do not look too deeply into the cold reflection of the mirror, my love. For your eyes are not yet trained to see the true depth of your beauty or to read the glorious tales of your imperfections.

Look instead into my eyes as I gaze upon your everything, and learn what it truly means to be loved for nothing more than the pure essence of your being.

Please, my love, try to see yourself as I do –
as someone worthy of complete and utter adoration.

GOLDEN GRACE

You can love her
but I beg of you, please,
do not try and own her.

She is the epitome of everything
that is wild, free and beautiful in this world
and wild things should not be caged –
for no one has the right to selfishly keep such beauty
from touching the world.

Confining her heart and taming her spirit
would be a fate far worse than death.
It would be the ruin of everything
that makes her so unique, precious and raw.

So, let the sun kiss her skin
and the breeze be her only guide
as she spreads her wings and flies.

She was not made to fit the molds,
nor be contained by greedy hands.

She was born to shine and soar –
to remain completely unrefined and pure
in her golden grace.

So, you may love her,
but do not try and own her –
allow her the freedom
that makes her so truly beautiful in her own right.

REAP WHAT YOU SOW

If you seek peace,
be still.
If you seek wisdom,
be silent.
If you seek love,
be yourself.

Not So Sweet-Sixteen

"Despite the way I feel about my life, I know I can find beauty in whatever you show me. Even my body, scarred and torn, has value. For our scars have the power to remind us that the pains of our past are real and the ability to tell stories we have not the courage to speak. I am grateful for every scar I have and they will forever remind me of the truth. Remind me that there is something in this life worth fighting for as they are my way to keep on living. They are the only part of my life in which I have no concerns, no hate. They are mine and I choose to cherish what no one else will ever understand"

ABSOLUTION

I know that life can hurt, my dear,
but you must find a way to cope and heal
each and every time that you break.

For if you hold onto any hurt for too long
it has a malicious way
of transforming itself into sullenness and anger.

So, I beg of you, please,
when you are left with open wounds
learn to bleed forgiveness
in place of bitterness and pain.

Forgive for the sake of no one but yourself –
for forgiveness heals the soul, frees the mind
and unburdens the heart.

Forgiveness is the greatest gift
that you can bestow upon yourself.

Embittered hearts
cease to live a life
fit for humanity.

RENAISSANCE

I woke this morning with a riot in my heart
and revelation echoing through my bones.

My soul was screaming for renaissance –
begging me to shed the weight of a past
that does not define me
and step out from beneath the burden of insecurities
that do not truly belong to me.

Begging me to bud, bloom and blossom
in all the places I too long hid and neglected.

So, watch now as I grow beyond the meaningless –
watch as I am reborn into myself.

TACTILE

There is so much blindness in sight.
The way that we choose only to see
what we can see.

So darling,
close your eyes.

Close them to the lies
they show you
and dare to feel my soul
rather than gaze upon my mask.

WILDFLOWERS AND WEEDS

Do not stroll peacefully through
my wildflower fields
nor wade gently in the cerulean shallow
of my shores
and speak sweet words of love.

For it is too easy
to find reverence
whilst amongst my beauty
and in my calm.

You see, my light (my luster)
is glorious.

I burn brilliantly bright
and I can (will)
illuminate your world,
but what will you do
on the days when my flame falters?

On the days that my fields
are made more of weeds and thorns
and my shore is buried
beneath turbulent, tumultuous depths?

Will you still speak those sweet words,
or will bitter poison
drip instead from your lips?

So, hold your tongue
in my wildflower fields
and cerulean shallows
and do not promise me anything
until you have fallen in love
with my absolute everything.

SEASONAL TRUTHS

Too often do I write of happiness,
of contentment, peace and endless summers –
but please do not make the mistake
of believing that is where I always live.
It is my home now, yes,
but still do I visit the cold winter of dejection
and swim the drowning depths of anxiety.
Still do I know uncertainty
and have my moments of doubt,
of that you can be sure.
I am not infallible. I am not impenetrable.
I am not something more
than the wonder that is humanity.
I simply know that now I have found my home,
my true home,
never will I venture too far
that I will lose sight of my truths.

MY LEGACY

For too long did I crave the superficial – longing only for grandeur, admiration and praise. Wanting so desperately to be seen, to be thrown longing glances from ever lingering eyes. To be worshipped and loved for the arbitrary rather than the substantial.

But now, I'd rather be known for my words than my face, appreciated for my mind instead of my body and remembered for something more than that which is transient and ultimately inconsequential.

Now I want to be felt, wholeheartedly and intensely. I want to burn on in the hearts of those whose paths I have crossed and in the minds of those whom my words have touched. I want to be remembered for nothing more than these words of truth and hope.

My name does not need to stand the test of time. I am more than willing to let it burn away quickly or settle quietly upon a dusty shelf to be forgotten. But in my heart of hearts I hope that the passion I breathe into my life and try to imbue within others will find a way to defy the odds and become eternal.

FOREVER ENOUGH

They look at me and see strength. And so they have told me, time and time again, not realizing the weight they have placed upon my shoulders – the crippling expectations they have laden me with. They cannot see that under the pressure I am beginning to slouch, that cracks are starting to form and the foundations crumbling.

And whilst your smile shines so much brighter than these storms, I still have my moments of weakness when I falter and I fail. But I promise you that as long as you fight for me, I will be here – standing by your side and holding you up. I will find a way to weather this tempest and forever find a way to rise from the rubble I will repeatedly fall to.

I am no pillar of strength, not this infallible being they have labelled me, but I am your mother and that will forever be enough.

26.12.2017

Today...
Today I am broken
and there are no honeyed words I can find
to sugar-coat this pain.

I am trying...
Trying to tell myself that these hard times always
have a purpose
and that this senseless pain will not be in vain.

But sometimes...
Sometimes we are not better
for the chips in our hearts
and the bruises left upon our souls.

Sometimes the breaks do not heal stronger
and we are left needlessly fragile
and splintered rather than whole.

Tomorrow...
Tomorrow will be better (I promise).
It has to be better.

DIAMOND IN THE ROUGH

They tried so hard to break you,
and there were times
I almost thought they had.

But then I remembered your strength –
your utter resilience in the face of adversity.

I remembered that even when
you tore yourself apart
as despair ached down to your very marrow,
you survived.

Even at your gritty and bloody worst
you did not break yourself.

You survived the war within your heart and mind
and learned to flourish against all odds.

Baby, you are a force to be reckoned with,
so just let them try and break you
for we all know that diamonds are made under pressure.

HOME

Loving you
was the easiest thing I have ever done.

It was the thawing of my heart
after years too many spent in the chill of emptiness
that no other body could fill.

It was coming home
to the welcoming roar of fire
after spending a lifetime of aimless wander
in winter's cold embrace.

It was the returning to myself
after an eternity of being lost.

SEVERED

For years I have played puppet
to the wills of the world,
but no more.

I have begun to sever the ties
that bind me to anything but myself –
for my spirit was not made to be confined
by societal expectations
nor my heart contained by greedy hands.

I have found the strength within
to set myself free
and I will burn as brilliantly as I desire
or as slowly as I please –
finally, I will be at peace with everything
that is, and is not, me

LUNAR

The moon is a powerful reminder that we can be beautiful no matter how much of ourselves we choose to bare.

That we can be cherished even when we change – when we regress and when we grow.

That each of our phases are worthy, but we are at our most remarkable (unforgettable) when we are full and wholly ourselves.

WHISKEY KISSES

The turbulent waves of Winter
washed over her alabaster skin
just as the warm rays of Summer
kissed the crown of her chestnut hair.

Her heart blossomed in Spring
and the parts of her life and self
that she had outgrown shed and changed in Autumn.

And, gracefully, she embraced it all,
for she knew that she could not appreciate
the true beauty of light
without the powerful contrast of darkness.

She knew that peace
was about finding contentment within imperfection
and forever embracing disparity and pandemonium.

And so, she took the good with the bad
and the bad with a shot of whiskey –
a constant reminder that what can burn at first
can later warm the belly of your soul.

REDEMPTION

I have been crippled by insecurities
and played slave to perfection's impossible allure.
I have broken myself
in order to try and appear whole
and withered myself
to better fit in the palms of others.
And, you see, it took breaking to the point
that I thought I was beyond mending,
beyond hope,
to realize that nothing (no one)
is ever too far gone to find redemption.
It was then I was reborn from my ashes
and was able to grow anew
from betwixt each and every crack.
It was then I learned that the ocean
does not apologize for its depth
and the mountains
do not seek forgiveness for the space they take
and so, neither shall I.

FEED THE WOLVES

Our whole lives we are told to feed the good wolf – to only embrace and demonstrate our refined, beautiful and humble qualities. And so, it is of no wonder that we grow up feeling disparate and incomplete. That we grow up not knowing how to wholly love ourselves.

For you must do so much more than simply feed the good wolf.

It is true that you must nurture him in his entirety, but you too must see and acknowledge the other wolf. For nothing in and of itself is inherently and wholly evil. You must accept and embrace him.

Do not neglect him, for in turn you are neglecting a part of yourself and it is the harsher, uglier parts of our beings that often need the most attention, care and nourishment. So, work with him, foster him and understand that he too has his role to play.

Remember that we are not beings of black and white, light and dark. We are contrast and we are nuance. We are beautifully complex and there is so much more to us than just the beautiful, calm and glorious.

Embracing our wild is one of the paths we must tread in order to find our true peace.

*There is something beautiful
about this untamed wilderness
we all harbor within.*

These unclipped wings.

This unfiltered roar.

Please know it isn't always graceful,
this learning to love,
this healing,
this looking in the mirror and smiling.

CREED

Do not be fooled, my dear, self-love is not an easy path to walk in this modern world. There will be those who dedicate themselves to cutting you down - trimming back your branches that they deem reach too far and pruning your flowers that dare to bloom brilliant.

This world will scream at you to be something more and somehow, still, so much less. It will ask you to forever want more when all you crave is to know contentment.

And even when you realize the beauty of what it is to love oneself and worship your being, there will still be times that a single kind or gentle thought eludes you and you are starved of worth.

This loving of the self is not something that once learned is never forgotten. It is a ritual that you must practice daily. A mantra that you must constantly repeat within the screaming silence of your mind. It is something that will take work, strength and more will than you think you have, but oh my, will it be worth it in the end.

YOUNG ONE

Thinking back to the girl I once was, that young girl of many a year ago, if I could tell her anything, anything at all, it would be this…

"Young One, there will be hard times – times harder than you will believe possible to survive and moments that you feel you have failed those dearest to you. You will face trial after tribulation and tribulation after trial, some of which will seem insurmountable – greater than life itself.

Yes, there will be hard times, but there will also be good times – times of love, acceptance, contentment and joy. Please, hold onto those times and know that no matter how often the hard and painful seem to outweigh the good and gentle, within you is something stronger than anything you will come to face.

For you are blessed with a spirit that burns with undying hope, the courage of a lion's mighty heart and wisdom beyond your tender years. And because of that not only will you persevere through the hard times and find a way to survive but you, Young One, you will bloom brilliantly, blossom beyond the boundaries of your despair and flourish against all odds.

But more than anything, Young One, I want to say 'thank you'. Thank you for never giving up on everything you were destined to become – everything that is now me.

For everything I am is due to your courage, wisdom and undying hope. And, for that, I am eternally grateful. So, thank you, Young One, thank you for helping me to become truly beautiful in my own right."

It isn't always pretty, this becoming,
but it will forever be beautiful
to those who understand.

About the Author

Becca Lee is a writer from Newcastle, Australia.

She writes only with the aim to inspire others to become their own inspiration, after having herself overcome the adversity of life's trials and tribulations. She writes of the beauty of imperfection, the complete contentment of self-love and the magic of undying hope.

Becoming Beautiful is her second collection of poetry and prose.

Instagram @beccaleepoetry

Facebook Becca Lee Poetry

Email beccaleepoetry@hotmail.com

Website www.beccaleepoetry.com

CPSIA information can be obtained
at www.ICGtesting.com
Printed in the USA
LVHW091131290519
619246LV00012B/661/P